JOHN ORTBERG
illustrated by Robert Dunn

your Magnificent Chooser

TYNDALE
K!DS

Tyndale House Publishers, Inc.
Carol Stream, IL

To Poppy Seed and Abby,
To Landon and to Claire,
To mothers and to fathers,
And to children everywhere.

Visit Tyndale's website for kids at www.tyndale.com/kids.

TYNDALE is a registered trademark of Tyndale House Publishers, Inc. The Tyndale Kids logo is a trademark of Tyndale House Publishers, Inc.

Your Magnificent Chooser

Designed by Jacqueline L. Nuñez

Edited by Stephanie Rische

For manufacturing information regarding this product, please call 1-800-323-9400.

For information about special discounts for bulk purchases, please contact Tyndale House Publishers at csresponse@tyndale.com or call 800-323-9400.

ISBN 978-1-4964-1742-8

Printed in China

23	22	21	20	19	18	17
7	6	5	4	3	2	1

Note to Parents

One day, a day you will never forget, you welcomed a beautiful little blob of protoplasm into your family. And watched the miracle of life growing.

One day, a day you will never forget, that little blob began to speak. And early on, you discovered that two of your child's favorite words were *no* and *mine*.

Your child was learning they have a will. This is very good.

But human wills—including the will of that beautiful little blob you brought home—get bent and twisted by selfishness and sin. That's very bad.

According to the Bible, having a will is part of what it means to be made in the image of God. The first assignment God gave human beings was to exercise dominion (Genesis 1:26). Each of us has a little kingdom—that sphere where our choices make a difference. We can say yes and no; we can create and decide. It's this core, God-given capacity that I call a "Chooser" in this book.

The shaping and training of the will—helping it to be strong and powerful in the service of the good—is one of the most important and most challenging tasks on earth. The reason this is such a challenge is because when your child was a baby, your will was always in charge. With a newborn, you can make all the choices to keep them safe and warm and fed and loved. But every day, your child's will gets a little more developed. Every day, your will must die a little. It's part of the long good-bye that begins so soon, that deepens on the first day of kindergarten and the first day of college.

This little book flows out of a book about choosing for adults called *All the Places to Go . . . How Will You Know?* So many of us grown-ups live our whole lives with a fear of making choices and missing out on God's will for our lives. But God made us to choose—and He wants to help us do it well. The deepest part of God's will for us is not the situations we inhabit but the people we become.

So what are you waiting for? You have a Chooser made in the image of our magnificent God. Let the choosing begin!

John Ortberg

God gave you two eyes,
Two ears, and one nose,
Ten wiggly fingers
And ten useful toes.

2

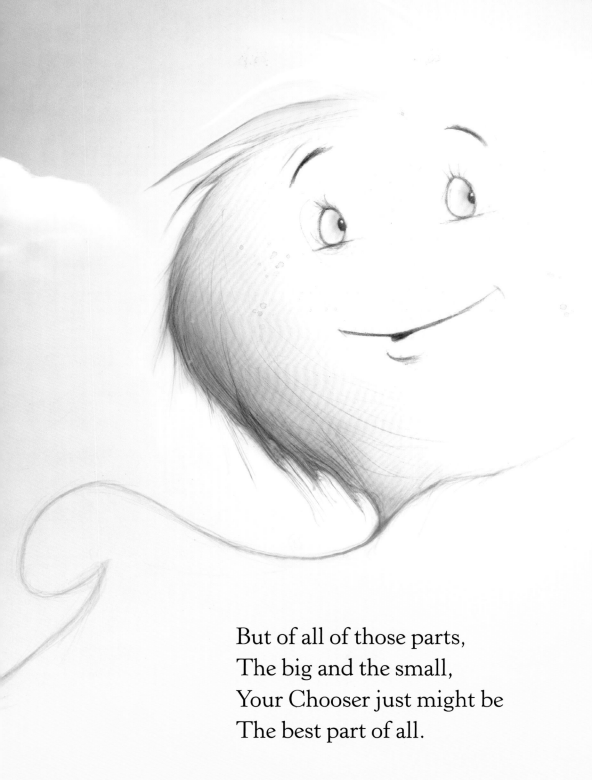

But of all of those parts,
The big and the small,
Your Chooser just might be
The best part of all.

A rock doesn't have one,
Nor does a tree,
But I'll tell you who's got one—
It's you! And it's me!

4

You can't really see it—
It's on your inside.
(For Choosers are shy,
And they quite like to hide.)

There are wonderful things
That your Chooser can do.
For your Chooser, you see,
Is what makes you just YOU.

6

Your Chooser says, "YES!"
And your Chooser says, "NO!"
And your Chooser says,
"There's someplace I'd like to go!"

7

And when it is dark,
And your prayers are all said,
Your Chooser says, "Nighttime's
The right time for bed."

8

Choosing's a cinch;
Anyone can learn how.
In fact, you can practice
Some choosing right now.

9

What will you wear
When you wake up—you choose!
Will you wear a blue shirt
Or some purple-y shoes?

Will you wake with a smile
Or start with a frown?
Your Chooser can choose
If you're up or you're down.

You can play with a friend;
You can read a good book.
You can go to the window
And just take a look.

12

You can choose what to say;
You can choose what to think.
You can go take a bath
So your feet will not stink.

Oh, I tell you, your Chooser's
A fabulous thing.
It can make you the boss!
It can make you the king!

But what if your Chooser
Does not get its way?
If your mom says, "Clean up"
When you wanted to play?

14

If your friend says, "That toy—
Could I use it awhile?"
But you don't want to share,
And you don't want to smile.

For a Chooser's a thing
That is not just for you,
Because everyone else
Has their own Chooser too.

17

If our Choosers collide,
Oh, what happens then?
Well, our Choosers can choose
To be friendly again.

We can choose to make up;
We can choose to be sweet.
For our Choosers can order
Our hands and our feet.

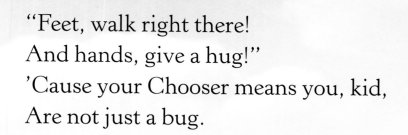

"Feet, walk right there!
And hands, give a hug!"
'Cause your Chooser means you, kid,
Are not just a bug.

You could use it to hit;
You could use it to shove,
But please don't, for the best way
To use it is love.

20

When your Chooser gets tired,
You can give it a nap.
And pretend that it's lying
Asleep on your lap.

You let it relax;
You give it a snooze.
You tell people, "I'm tired.
Now it's YOUR turn to choose!"

And after you've given it
Quiet and rest,
It will choose to choose more—
'Cause your Chooser's the best.

(When you use your Chooser
For longer and longer,
It only gets bigger
And better and stronger.)

Some people are scared
When it comes time to choose.
They're afraid they'll be wrong;
They're afraid they might lose.

So what if your Chooser
Goes and makes a mistake?
You're still not a loser;
You're still not a fake.

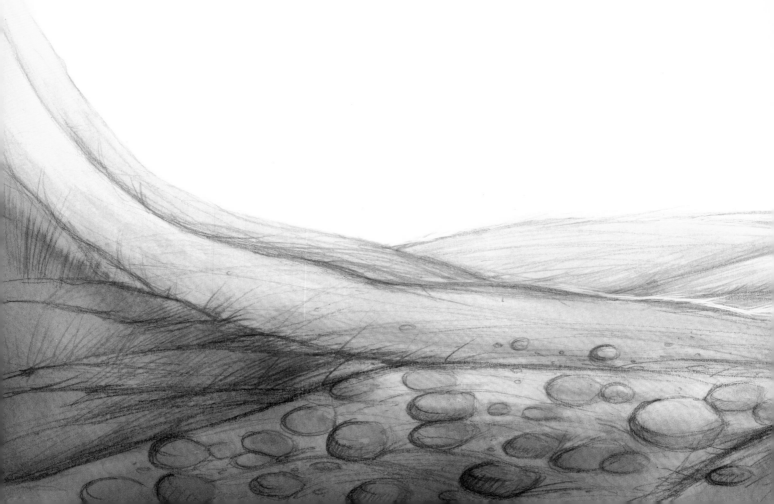

You can choose something new;
You can say, "This is when
My Chooser will choose
To start over again."

God gave you your Chooser,
So Choosers are good.
He wants you to use it
The way Jesus would.

Someday you'll grow up;
Then your Chooser will choose
Some exciting adventures
That might make the news.

You may climb a mountain
Or fly to the moon.
You might drive a car
Or a hot-air balloon.

But you won't lay some eggs,
Or go live in a zoo,
Because there are some things
Even a Chooser can't do.

Oh, your Thinker can think
(Which will make you quite smart),
And your Feeler can feel
(Which is good for your heart).

But your Chooser will choose
What you say and you do,
So your choosing is really just
Choosing up you.

Whenever you're stuck
And your mind fills with doubt,
You can just pray to God,
And He'll come help you out.

God knows about choosing
Up close and firsthand
For He has a Chooser—
The best in the land!

God's Chooser works better
Than yours or mine could.
His Chooser is perfect
And loving and good.

God didn't tell you
To sit there all day.
He wants you to choose—
So get on your way!

Now it's time to quit reading,
You choice-chooser, you,
And find something great
For your Chooser to do.

38